GUITAR SCALES
by

Introduction

The "Guitar Scales" didactic series divided into numerous booklets, is a great tool for study and master the scales, useful for both teachers and students. Each booklet deals with the study of a scale in all keys. Each scale is divided into five boxes and a fretboard map, where you can store notes horizontally and vertically. What are you waiting for? Start now!

Nocera Inferiore (SA) - Italy
For contacts:
tel. + 39 348 3471854
e-mail: abmanagement@libero.it

GUITAR SCALES:

THE LOCRIAN MODE

C LOCRIAN MODE

1 b2 b3 4 b5 b6 b7
C Db Eb F Gb Ab Bb

BOX 1

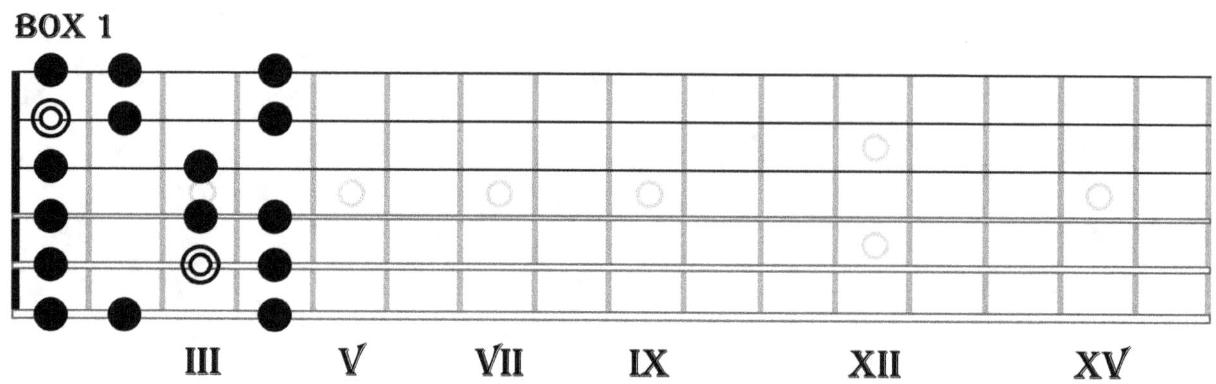

BOX 2

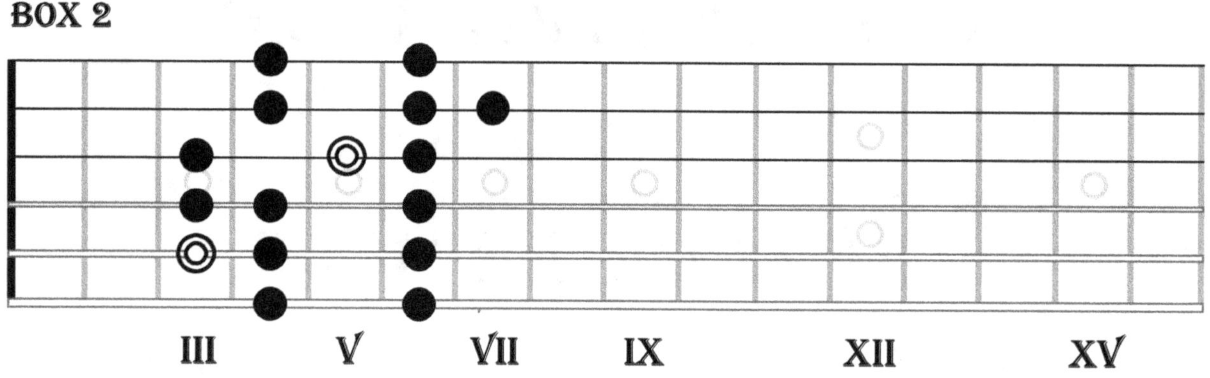

BOX 3

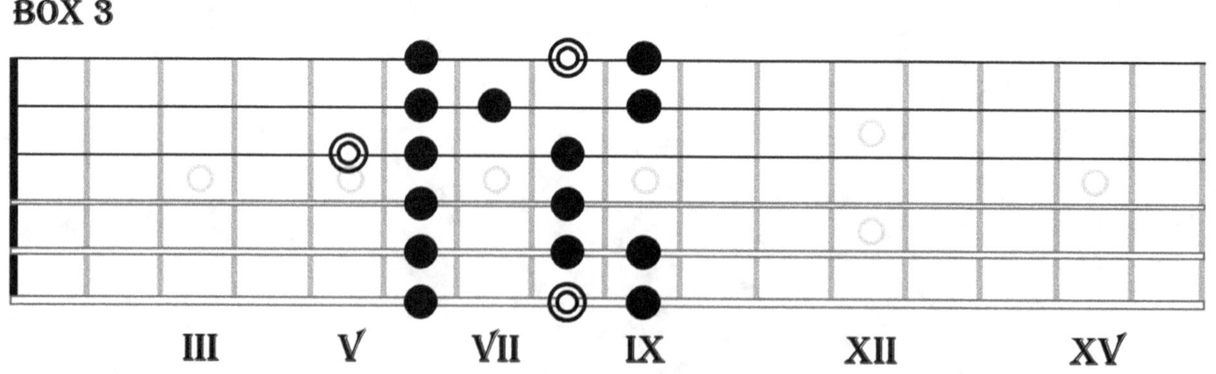

GUITAR SCALES: THE LOCRIAN MODE
BY LUCA MANCINO

BOX 4

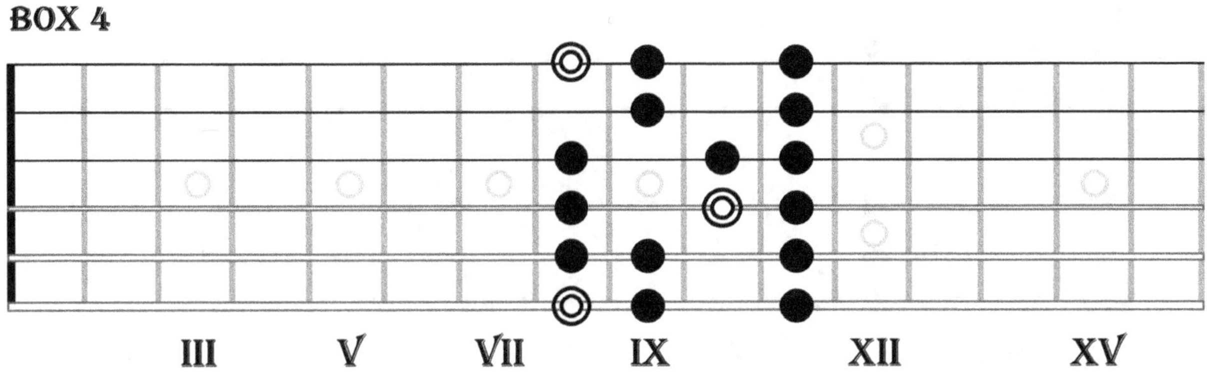

BOX 5

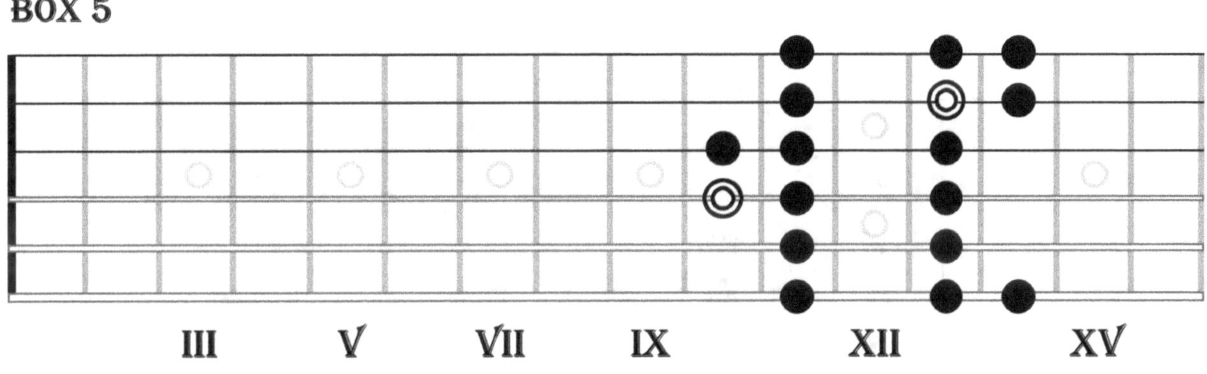

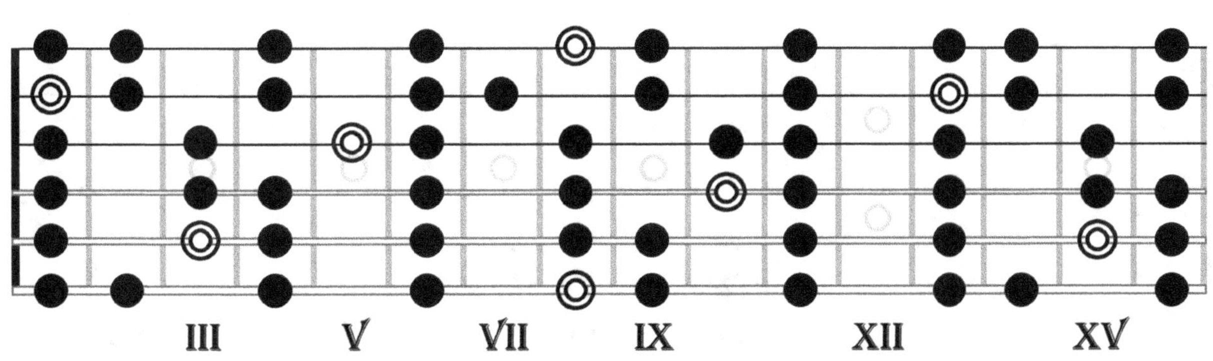

GUITAR SCALES: THE LOCRIAN MODE
BY LUCA MANCINO

C# LOCRIAN MODE

1 b2 b3 4 b5 b6 b7
C# D E F# G A B

BOX 1

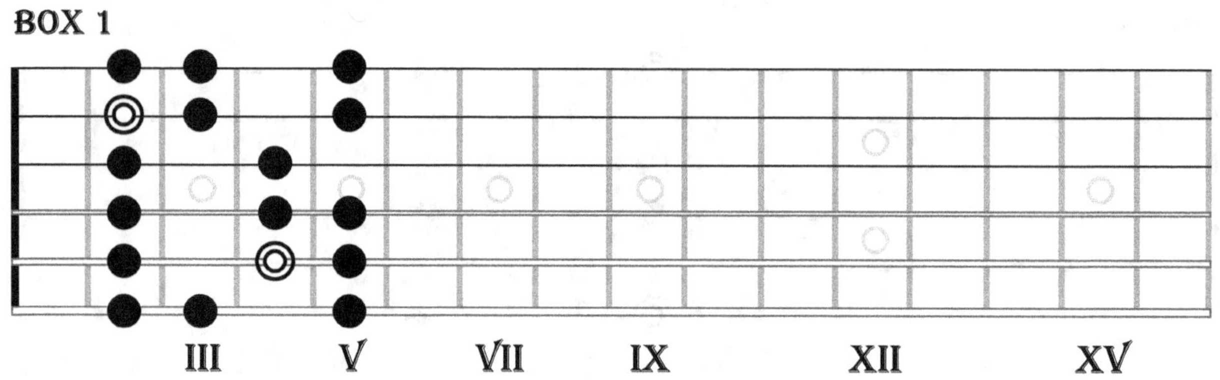

BOX 2

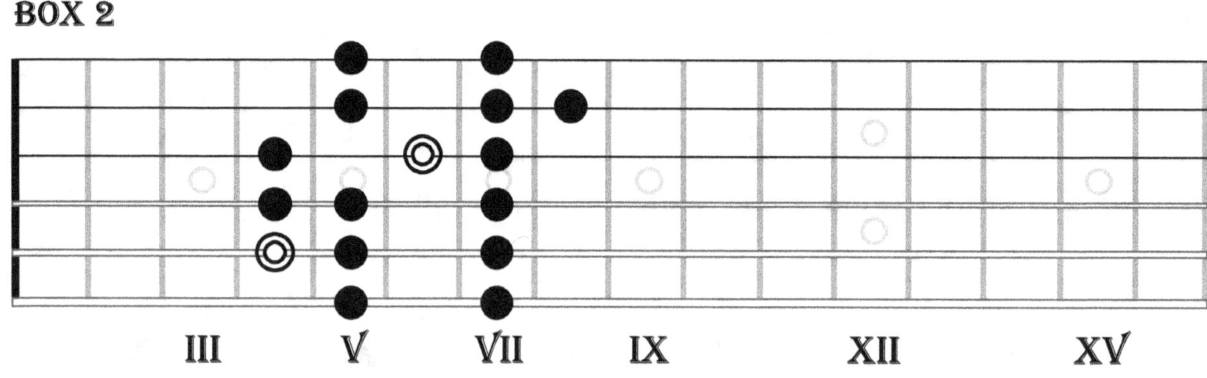

BOX 3

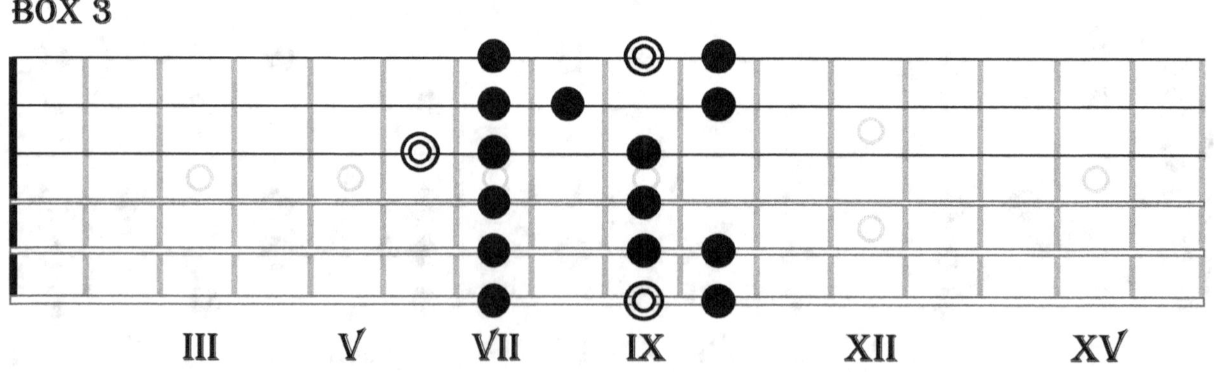

BOX 4

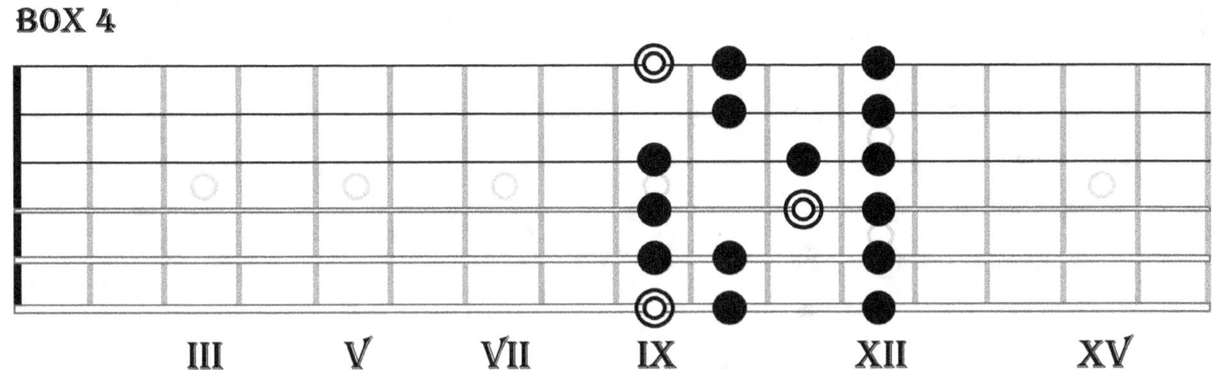

BOX 5

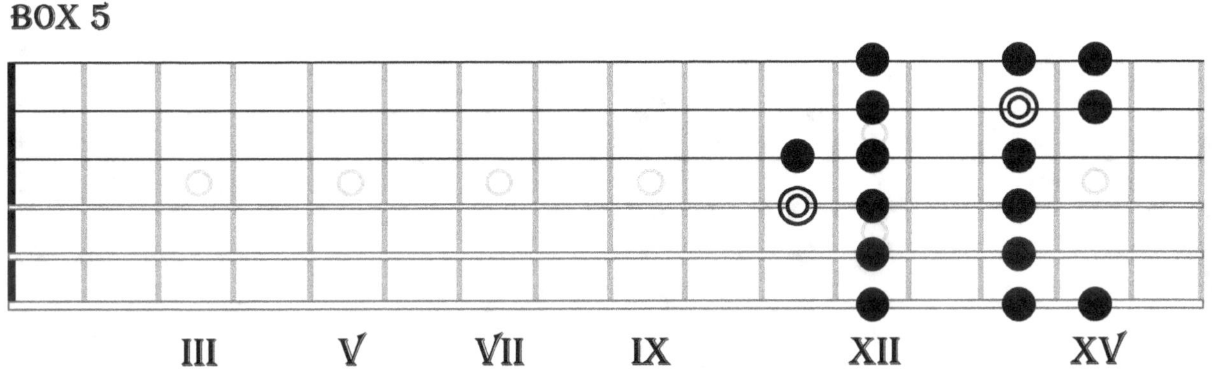

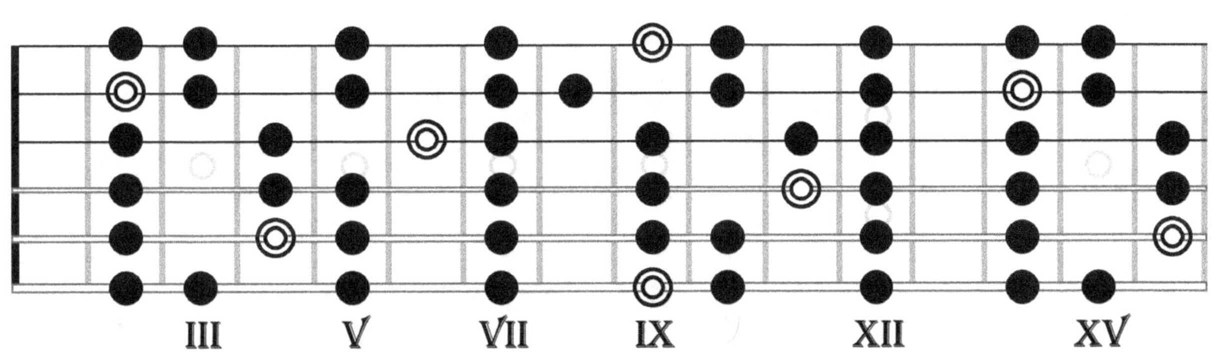

GUITAR SCALES: THE LOCRIAN MODE
BY LUCA MANCINO

D LOCRIAN MODE

1 b2 b3 4 b5 b6 b7
D Eb F G Ab Bb C

BOX 1

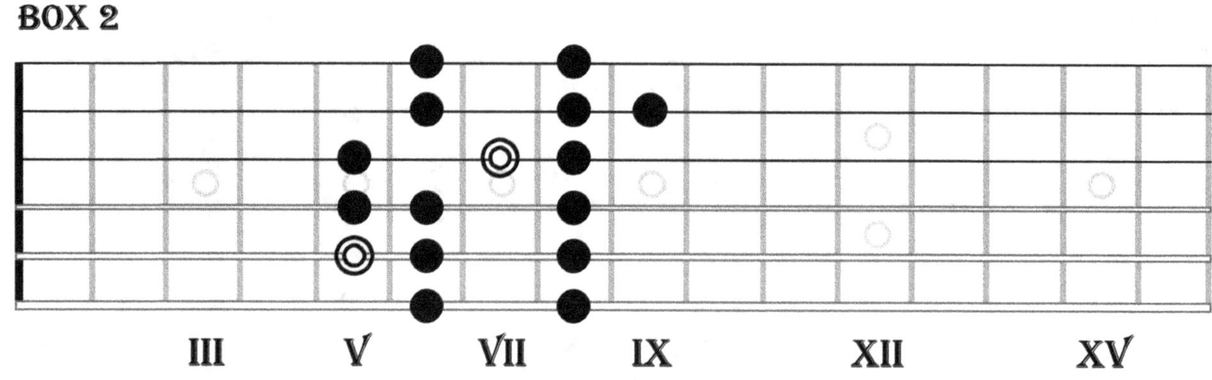

BOX 2

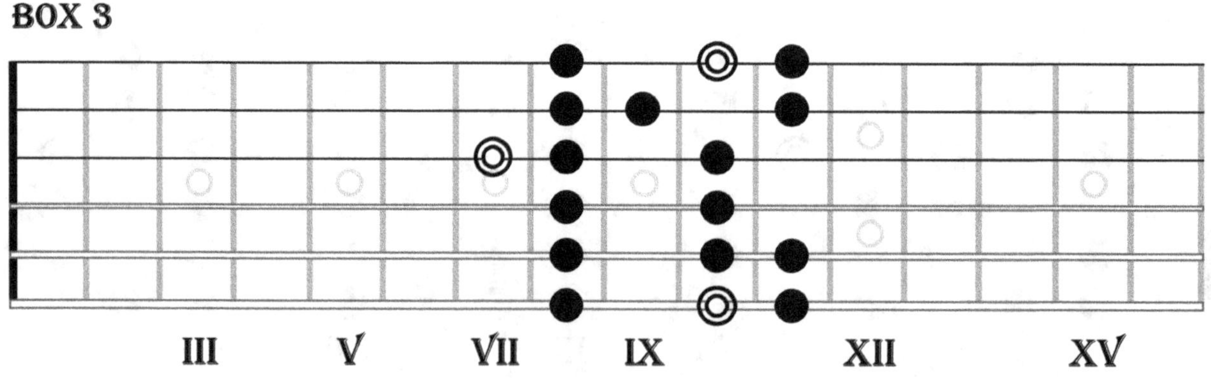

BOX 3

GUITAR SCALES: THE LOCRIAN MODE
BY LUCA MANCINO

BOX 4

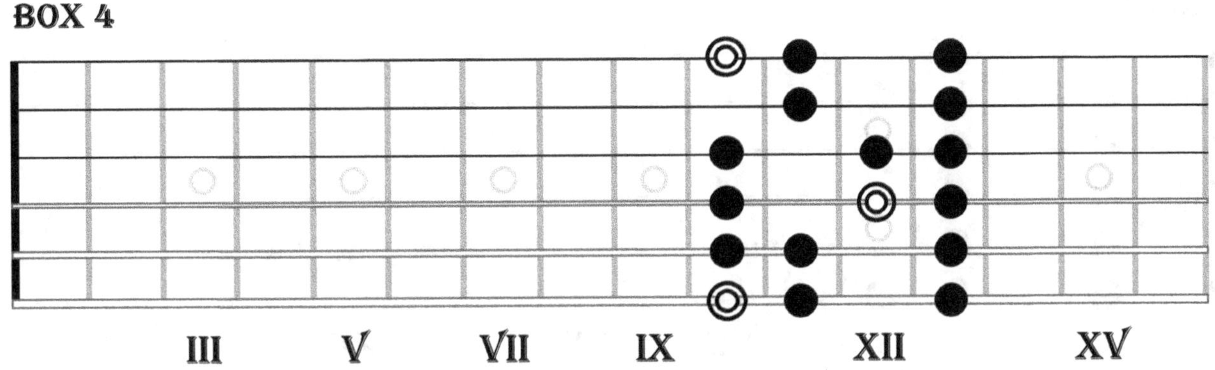

BOX 5

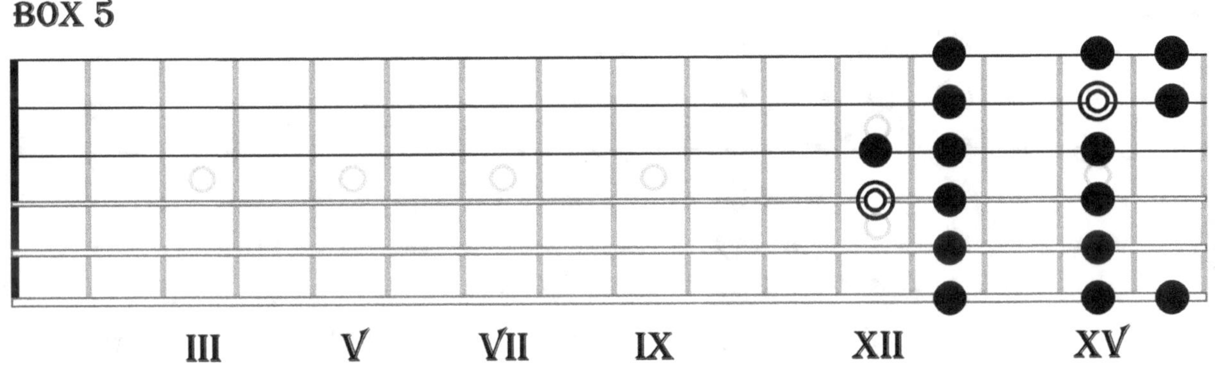

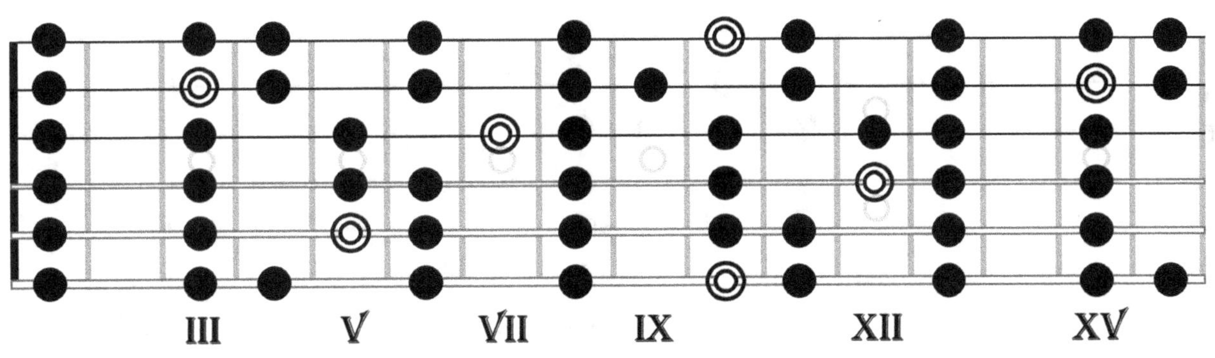

GUITAR SCALES: THE LOCRIAN MODE
BY LUCA MANCINO

D# LOCRIAN MODE

1 b2 b3 4 b5 b6 b7
D# E F# G# A B C#

BOX 1

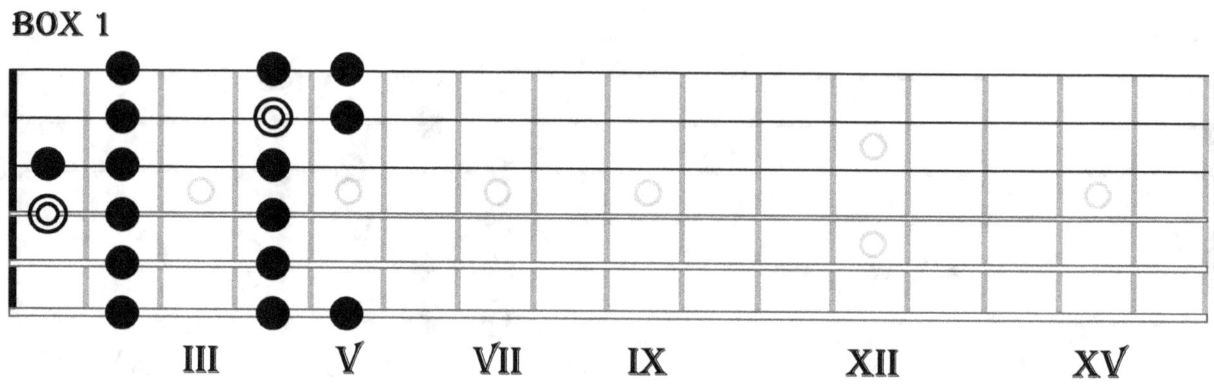

BOX 2

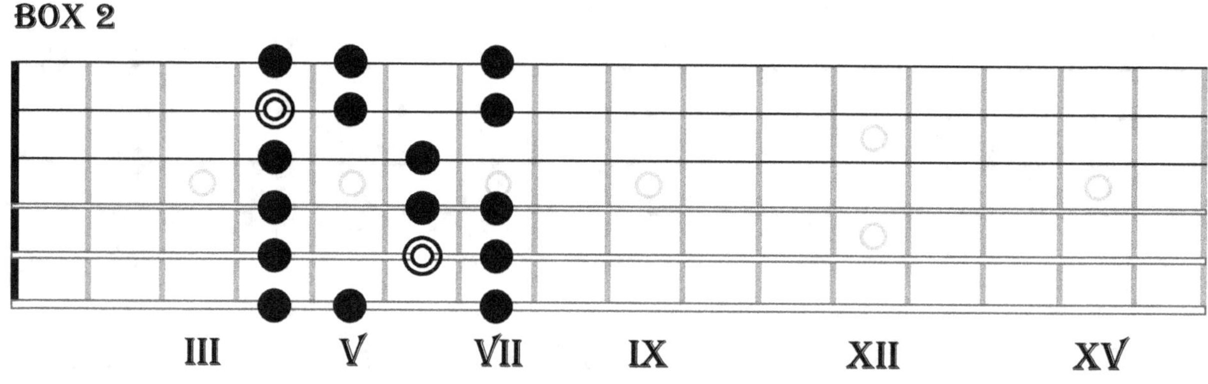

BOX 3

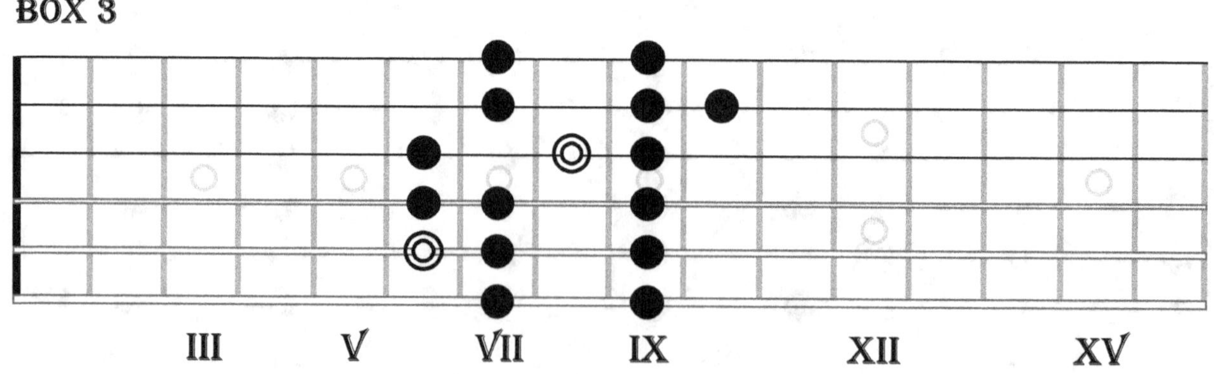

GUITAR SCALES: THE LOCRIAN MODE
BY LUCA MANCINO

BOX 4

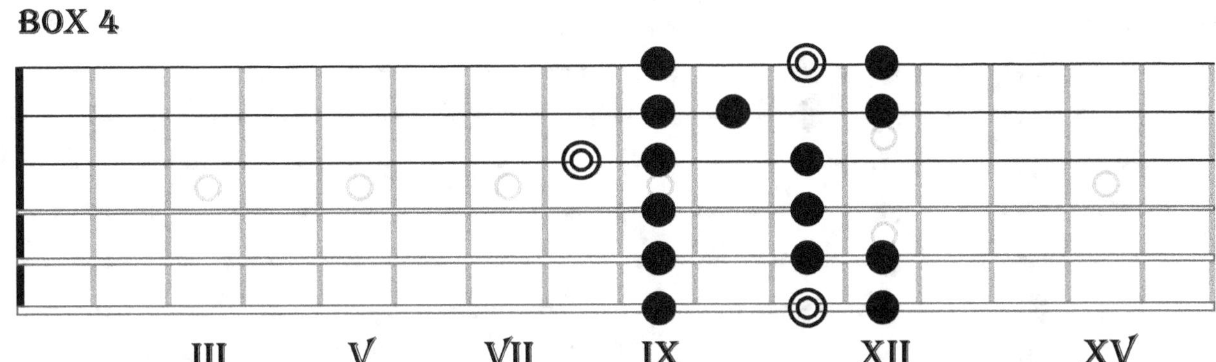

BOX 5

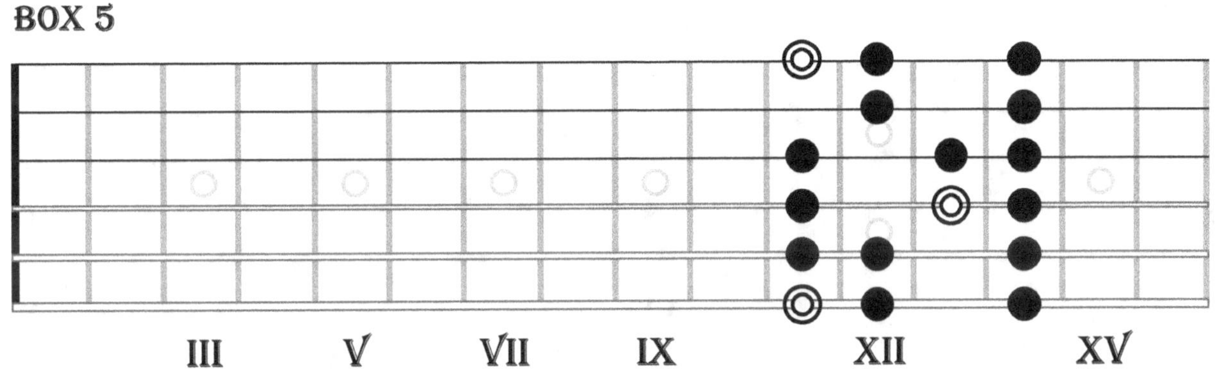

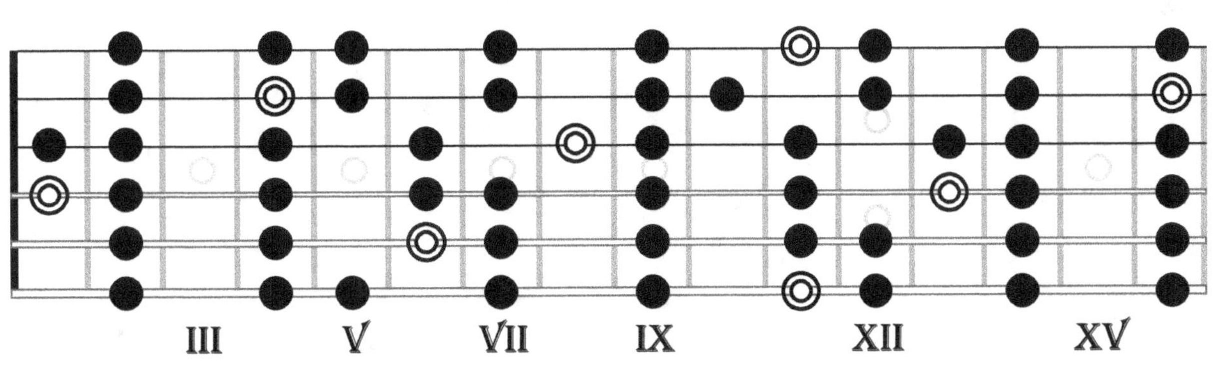

GUITAR SCALES: THE LOCRIAN MODE
BY LUCA MANCINO

E LOCRIAN MODE

1 b2 b3 4 b5 b6 b7
E F G A Bb C D

BOX 1

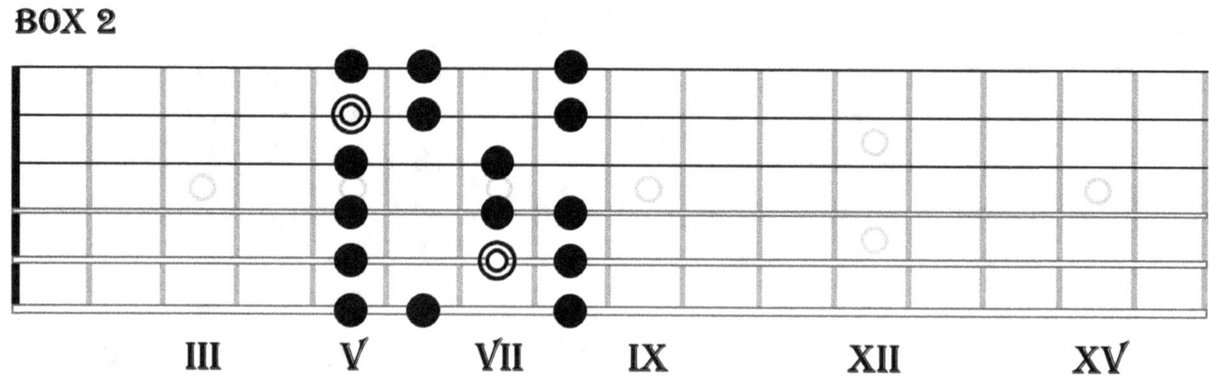

BOX 2

BOX 3

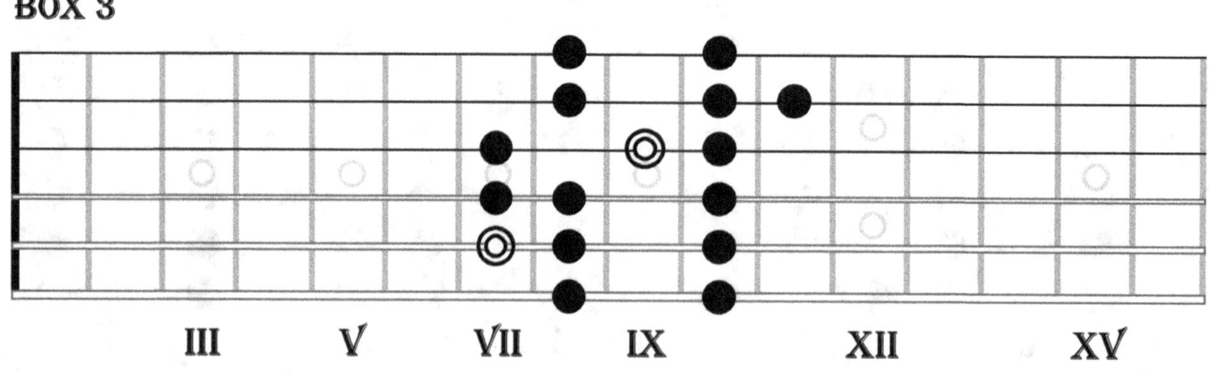

GUITAR SCALES: THE LOCRIAN MODE
BY LUCA MANCINO

BOX 4

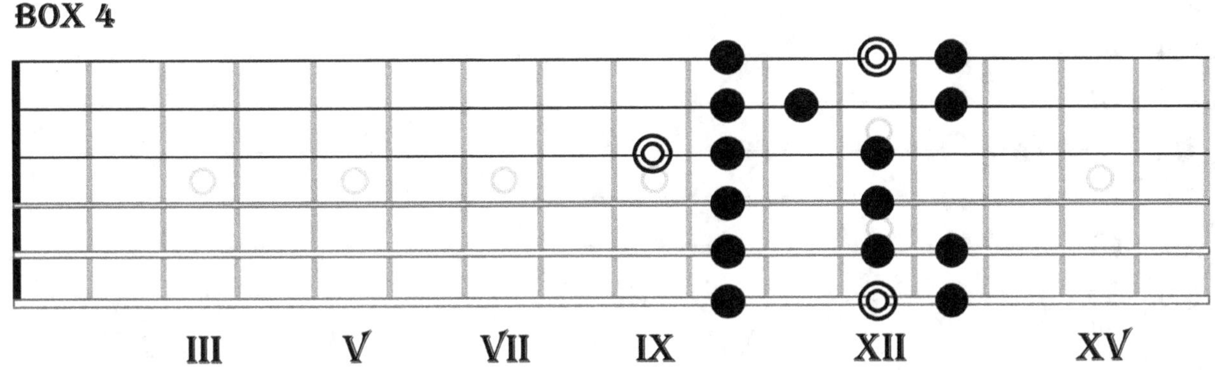

BOX 5

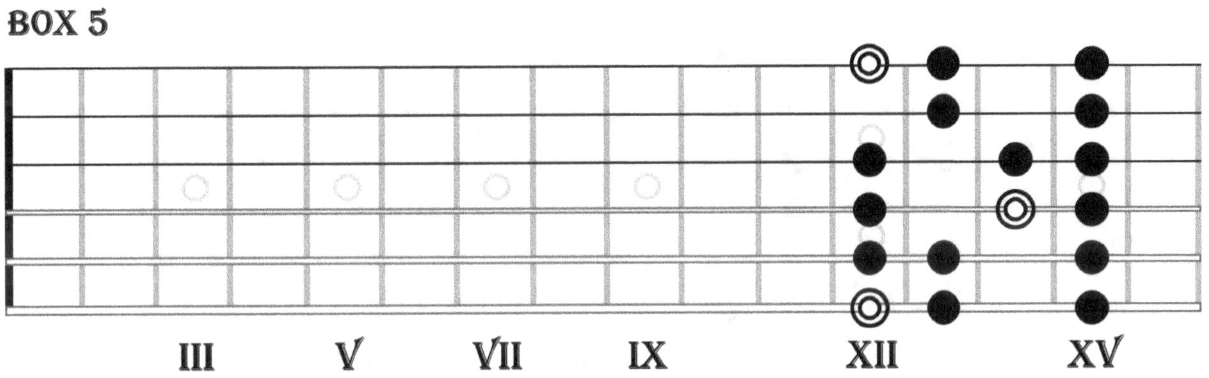

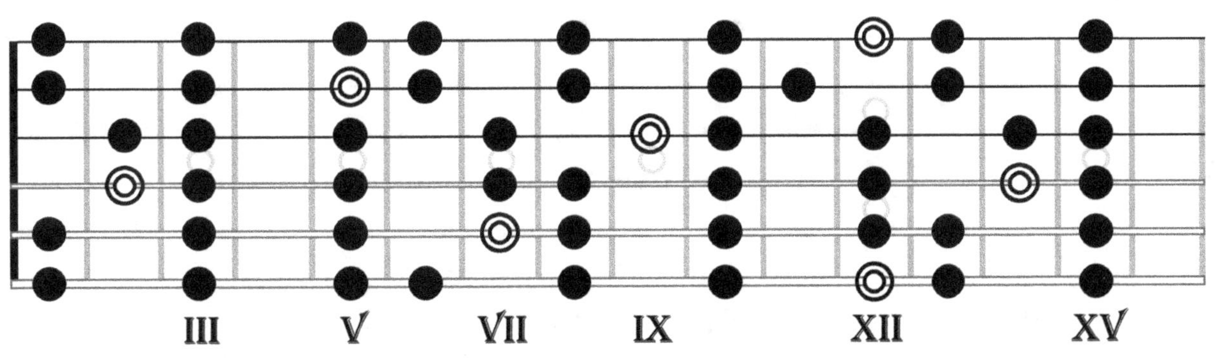

GUITAR SCALES: THE LOCRIAN MODE
BY LUCA MANCINO

F LOCRIAN MODE

1 b2 b3 4 b5 b6 b7
F Gb Ab Bb Cb Db Eb

BOX 1

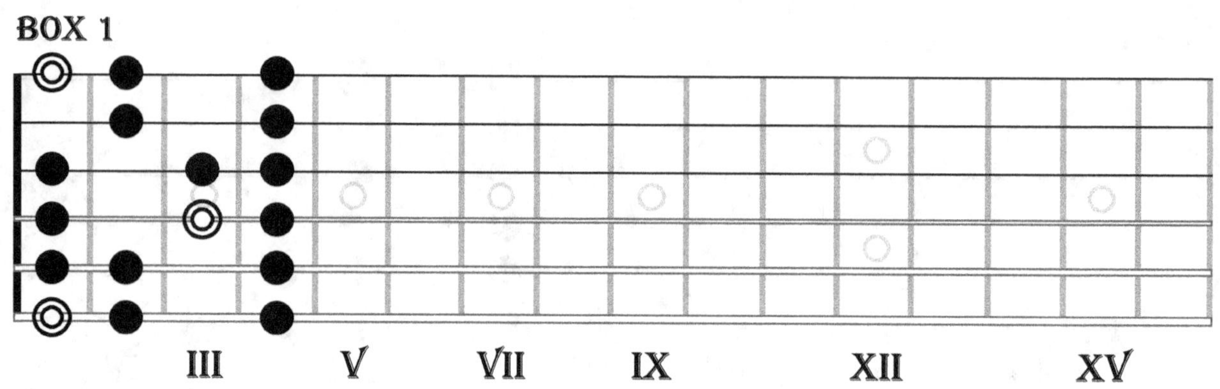

BOX 2

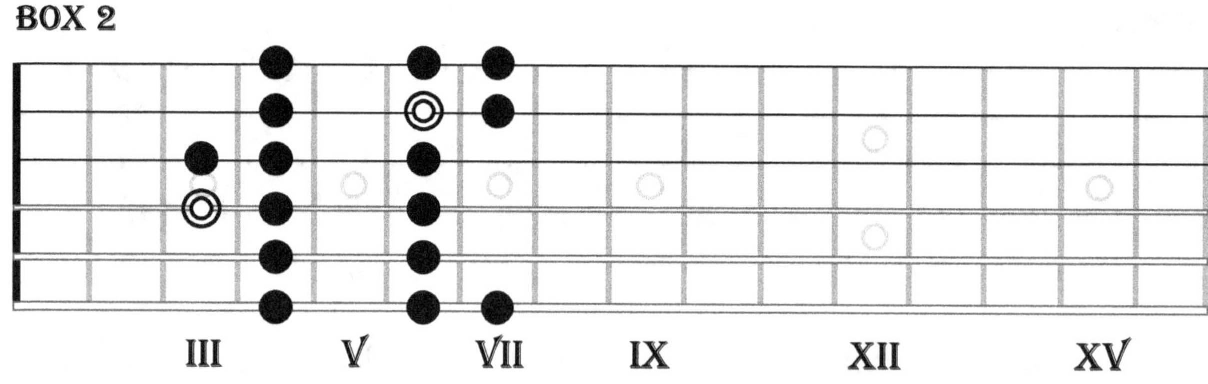

BOX 3

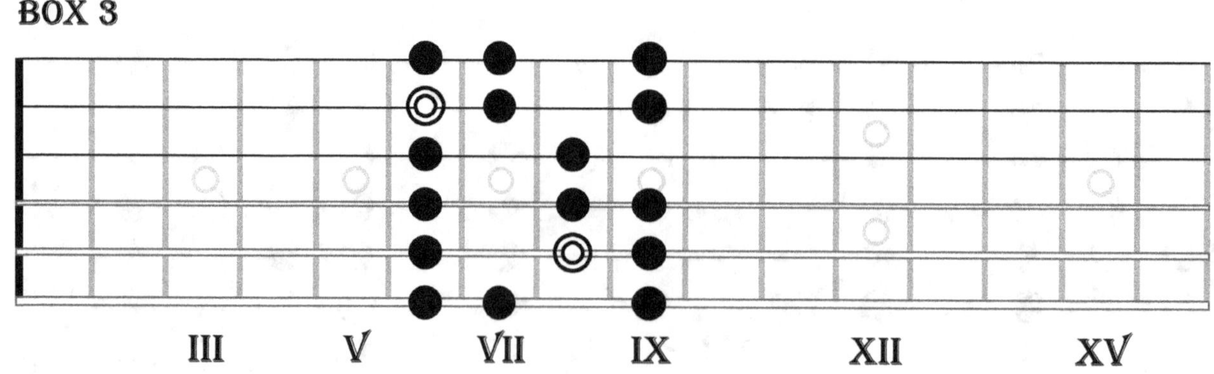

GUITAR SCALES: THE LOCRIAN MODE
BY LUCA MANCINO

BOX 4

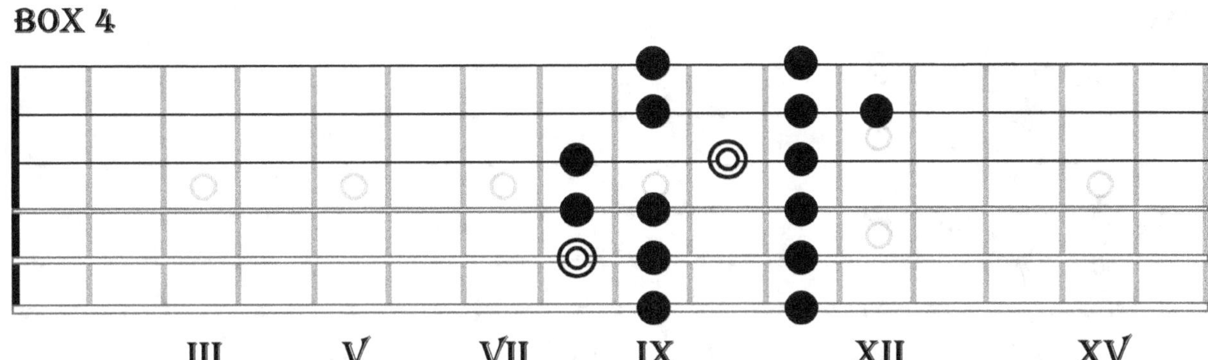

BOX 5

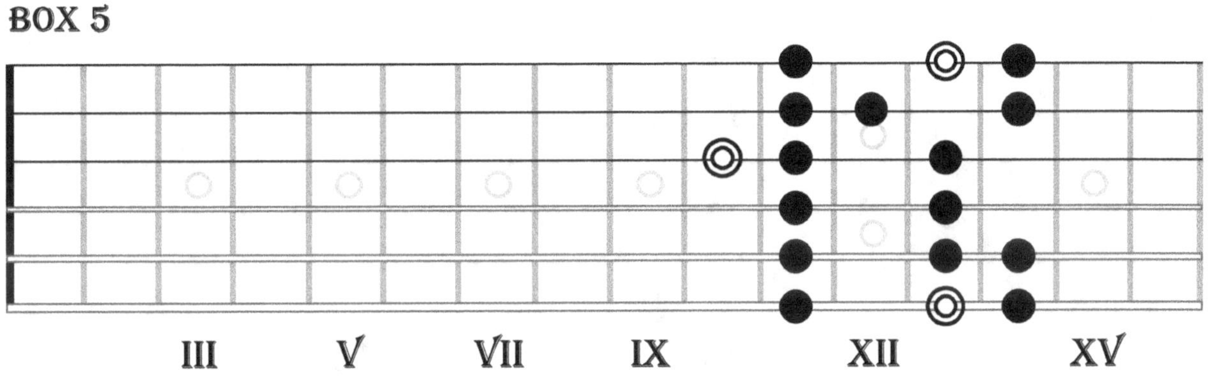

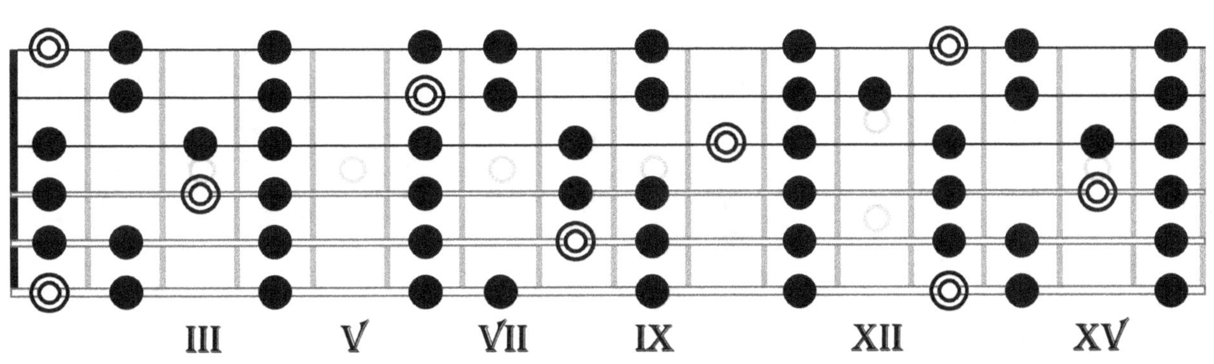

GUITAR SCALES: THE LOCRIAN MODE
BY LUCA MANCINO

F# LOCRIAN MODE

1 b2 b3 4 b5 b6 b7
F# G A B C D E

BOX 1

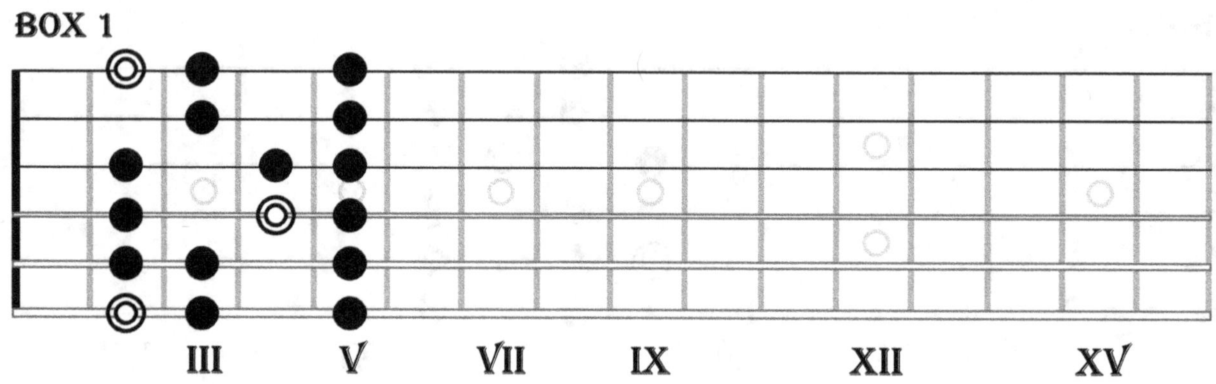

BOX 2

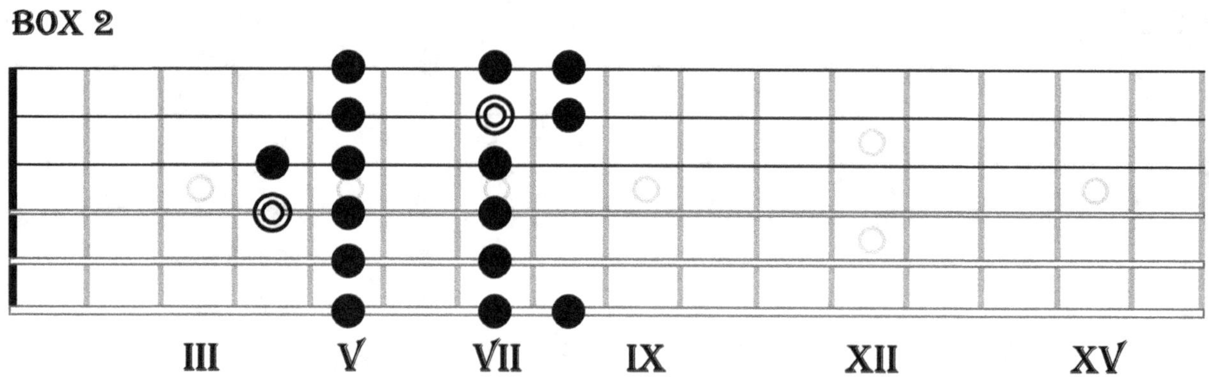

BOX 3

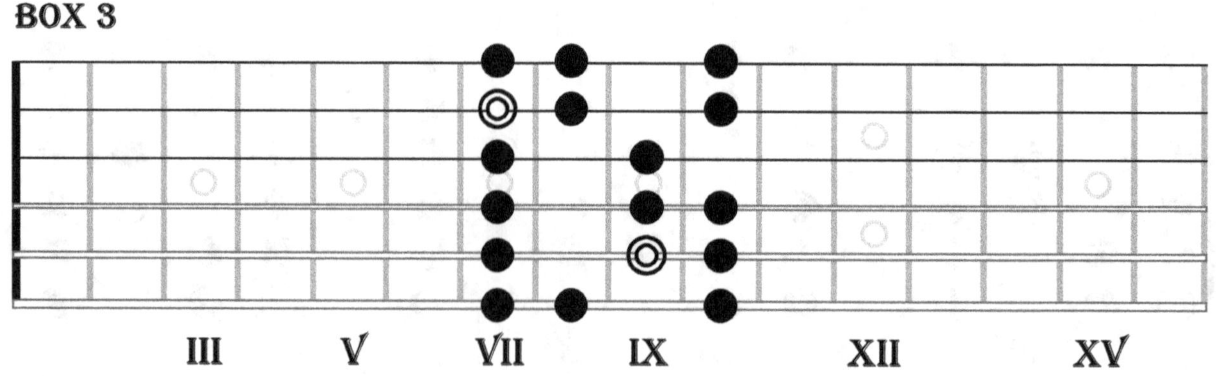

GUITAR SCALES: THE LOCRIAN MODE
BY LUCA MANCINO

BOX 4

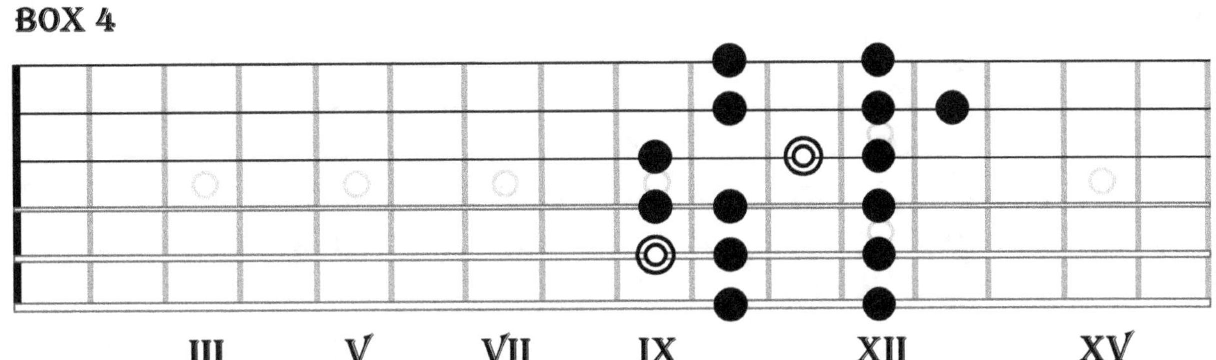

BOX 5

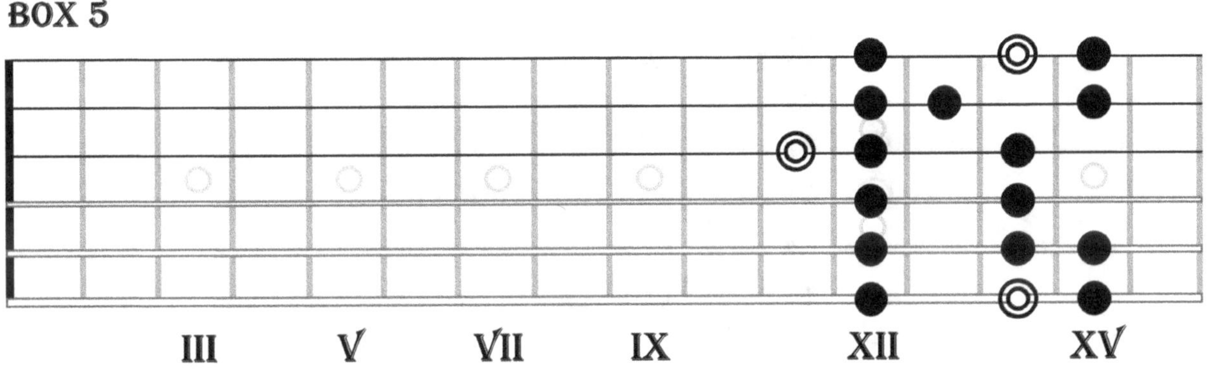

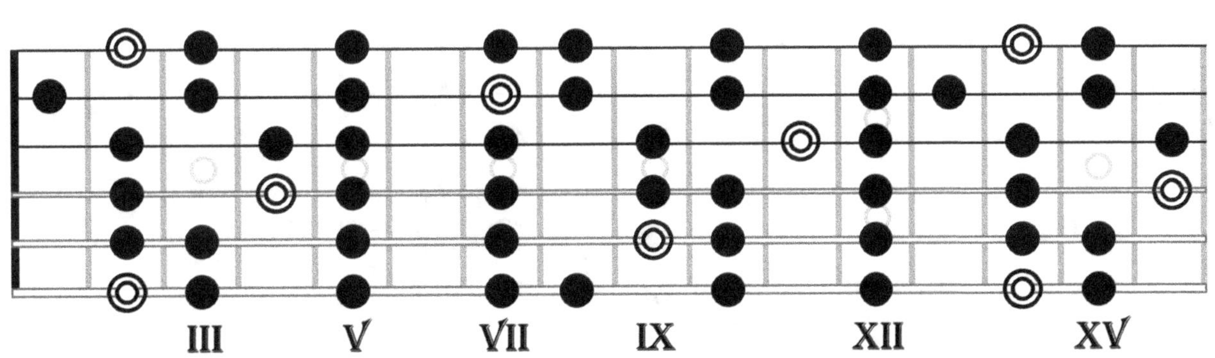

GUITAR SCALES: THE LOCRIAN MODE
BY LUCA MANCINO

G LOCRIAN MODE

1 b2 b3 4 b5 b6 b7
G Ab Bb C Db Eb F

BOX 1

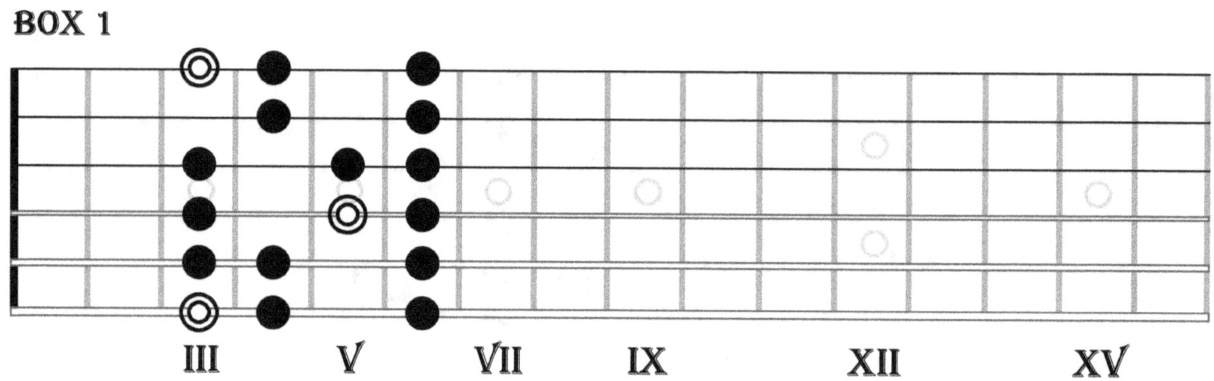

BOX 2

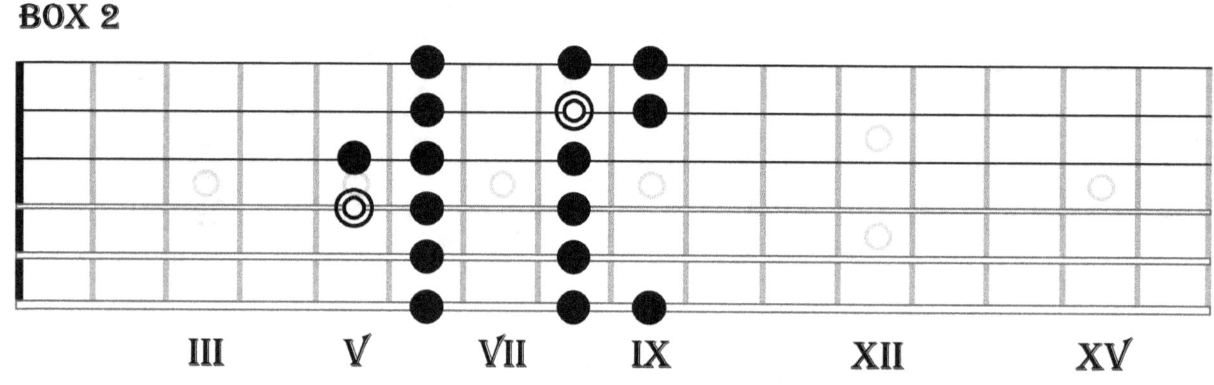

BOX 3

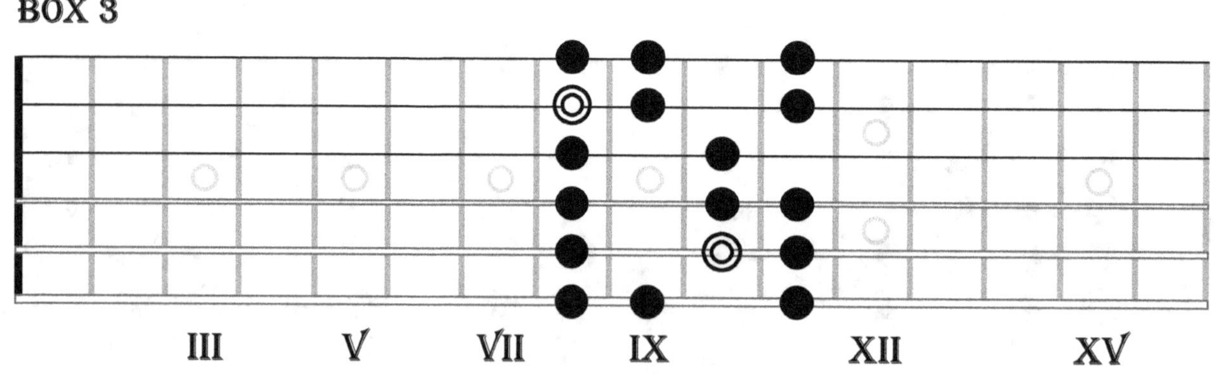

GUITAR SCALES: THE LOCRIAN MODE
BY LUCA MANCINO

BOX 4

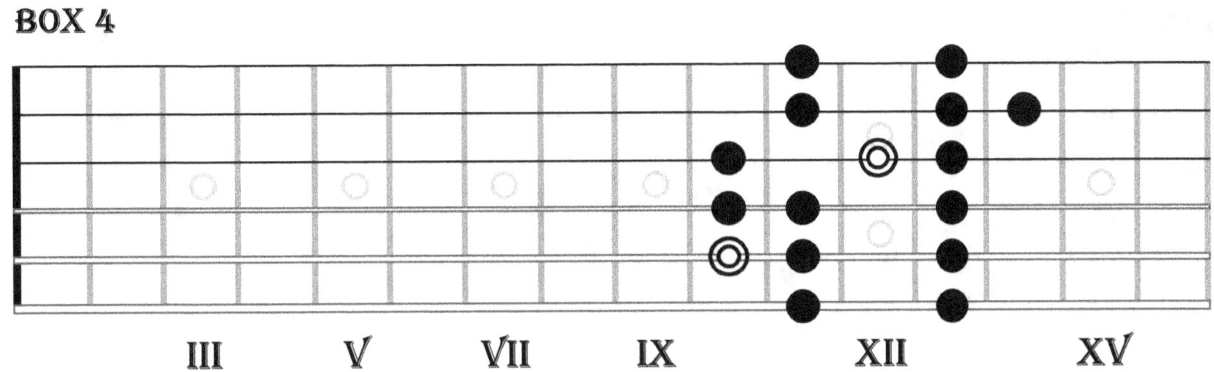

BOX 5

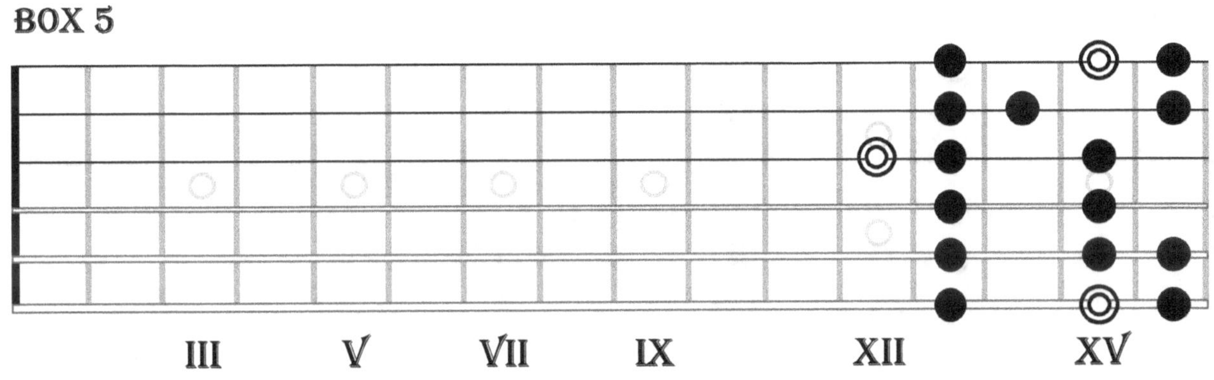

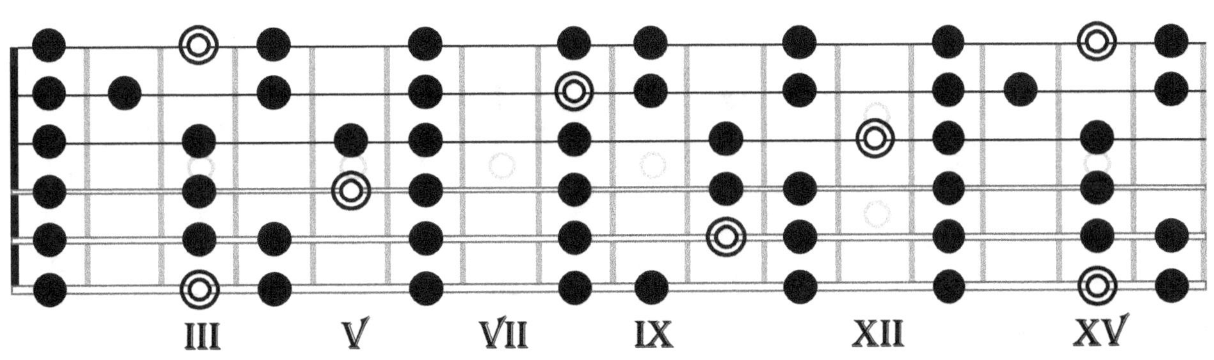

GUITAR SCALES: THE LOCRIAN MODE
BY LUCA MANCINO

G# LOCRIAN MODE

1 b2 b3 4 b5 b6 b7
G# A B C# D E F#

BOX 1

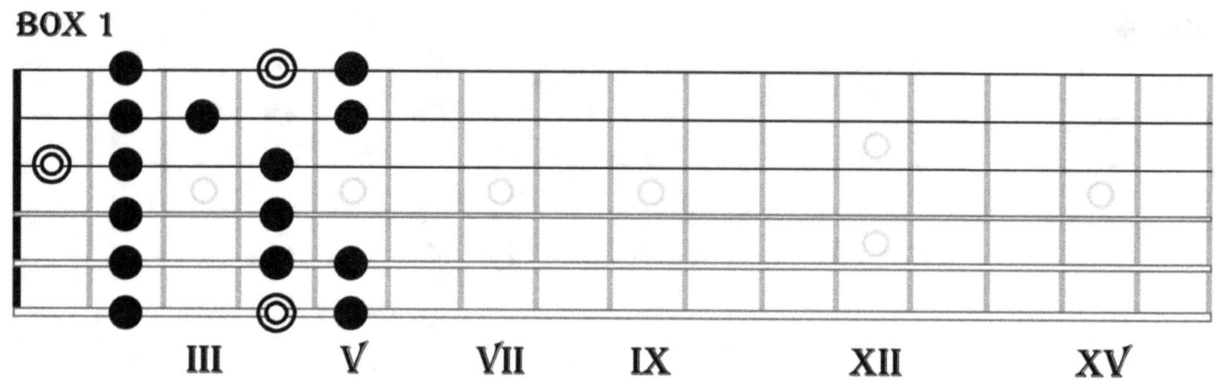

BOX 2

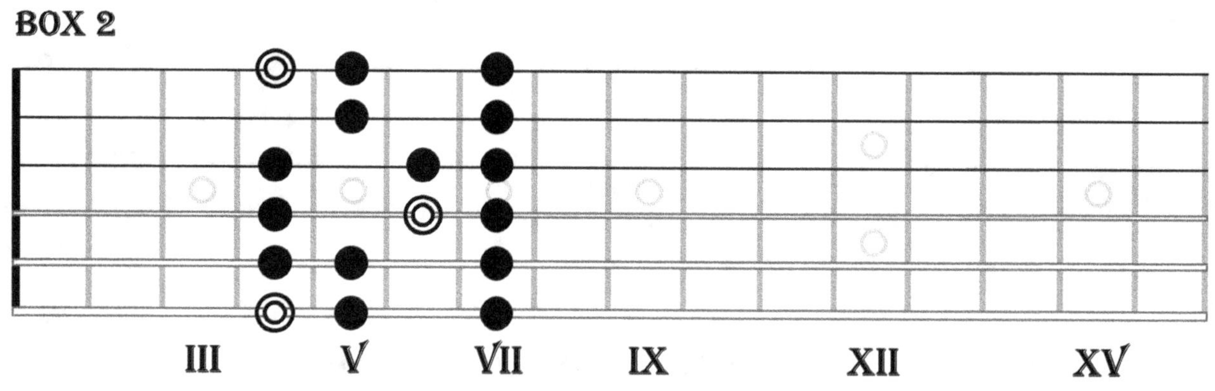

BOX 3

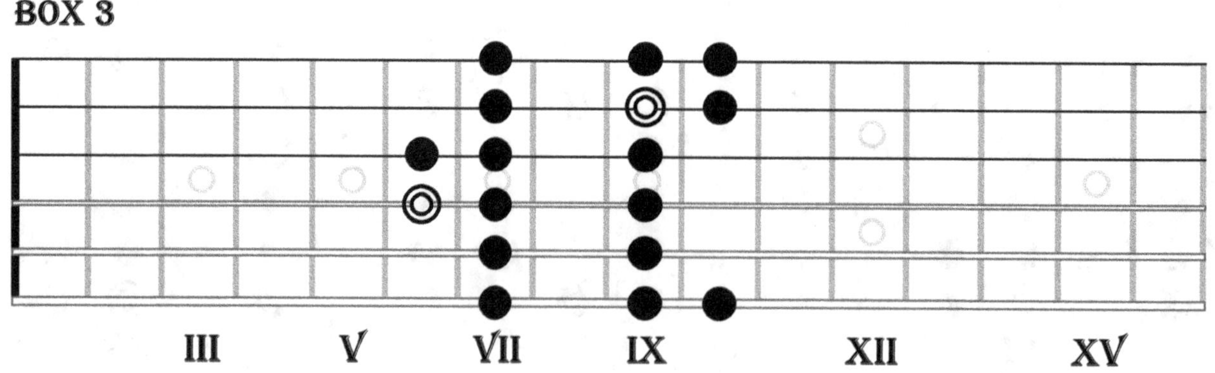

GUITAR SCALES: THE LOCRIAN MODE
BY LUCA MANCINO

BOX 4

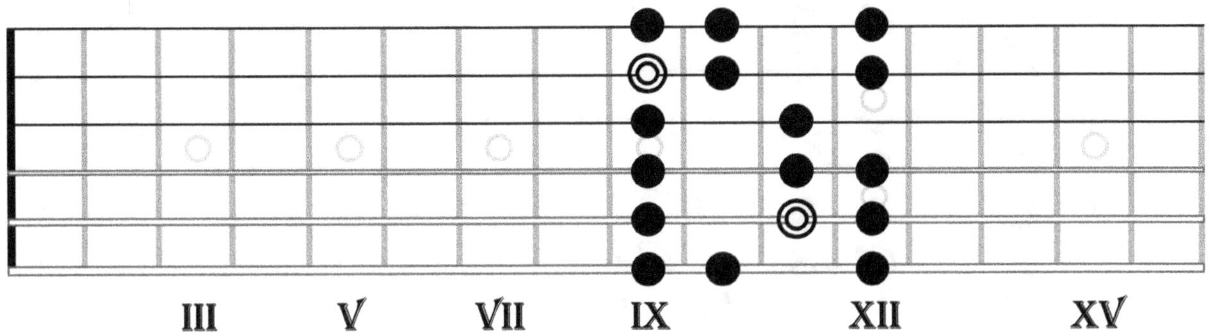

BOX 5

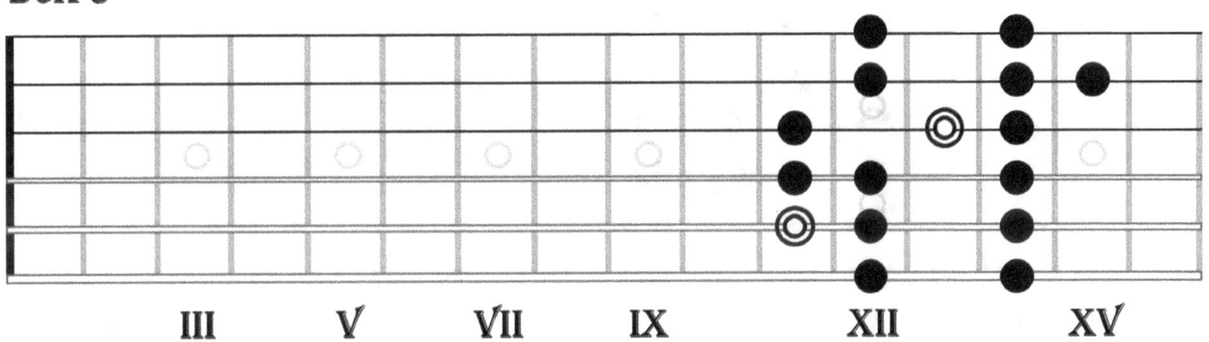

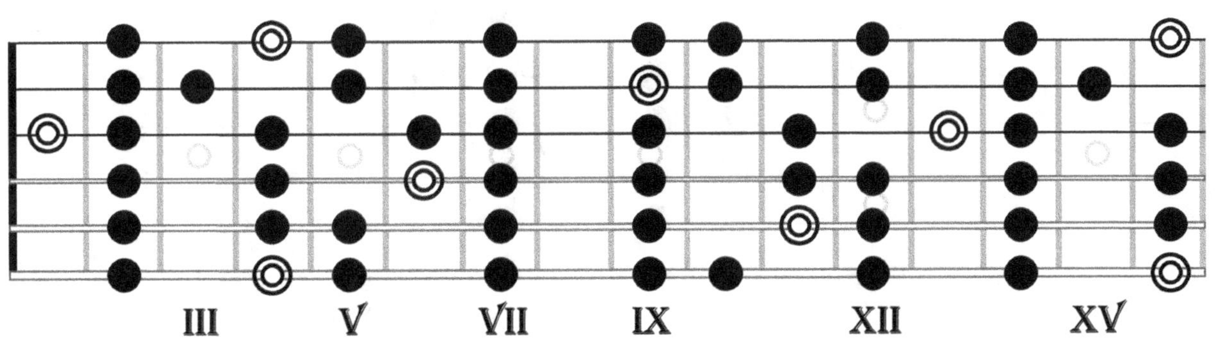

GUITAR SCALES: THE LOCRIAN MODE
BY LUCA MANCINO

A LOCRIAN MODE

1 b2 b3 4 b5 b6 b7
A Bb C D Eb F G

BOX 1

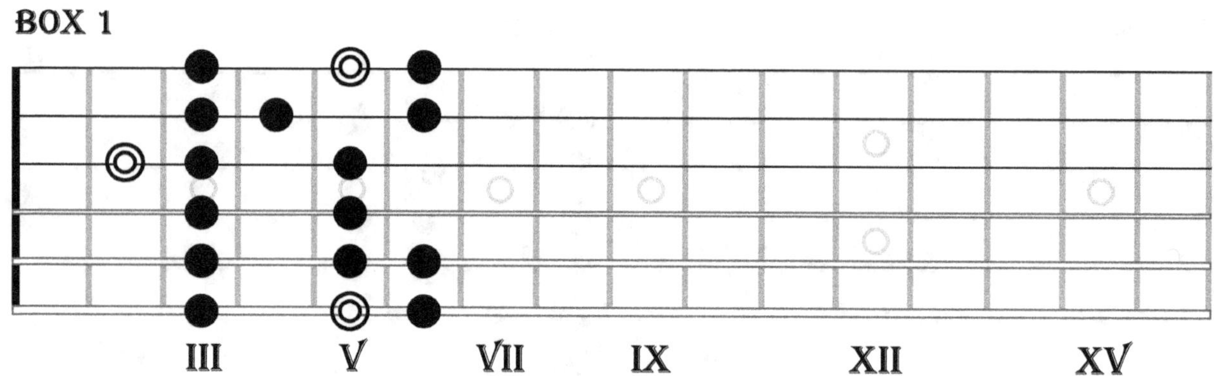

BOX 2

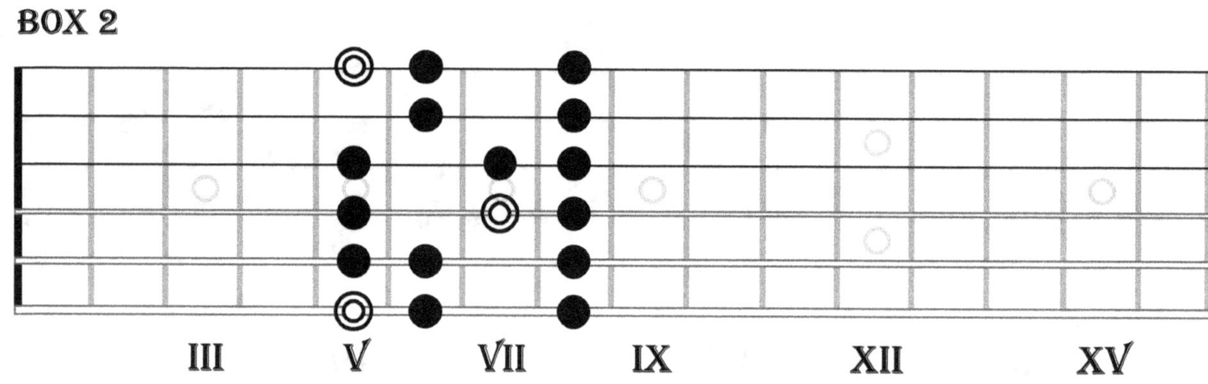

BOX 3

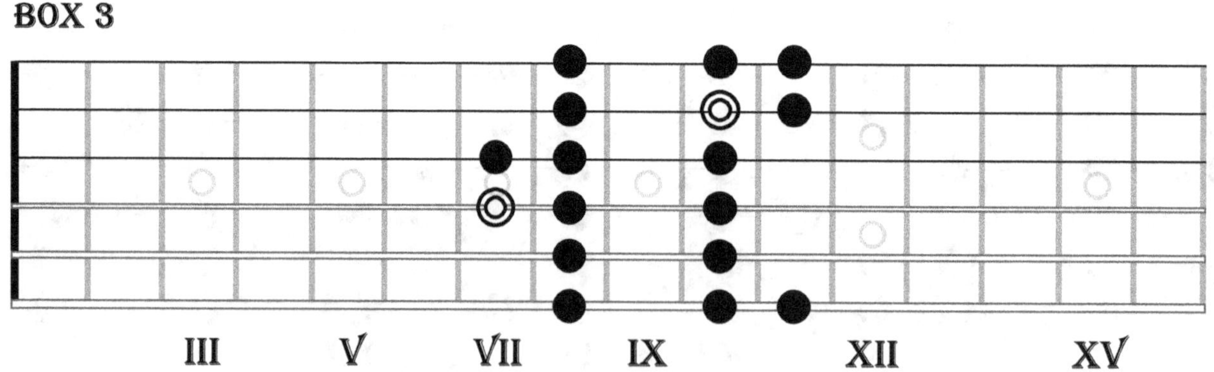

GUITAR SCALES: THE LOCRIAN MODE
BY LUCA MANCINO

BOX 4

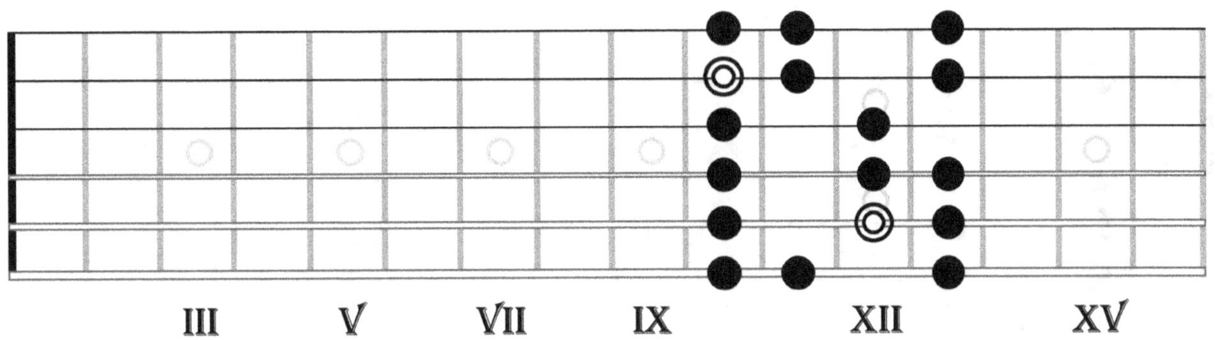

BOX 5

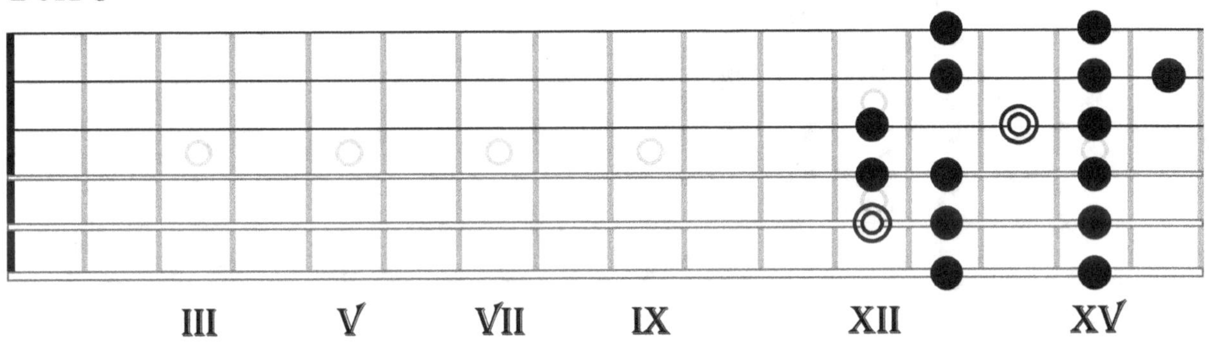

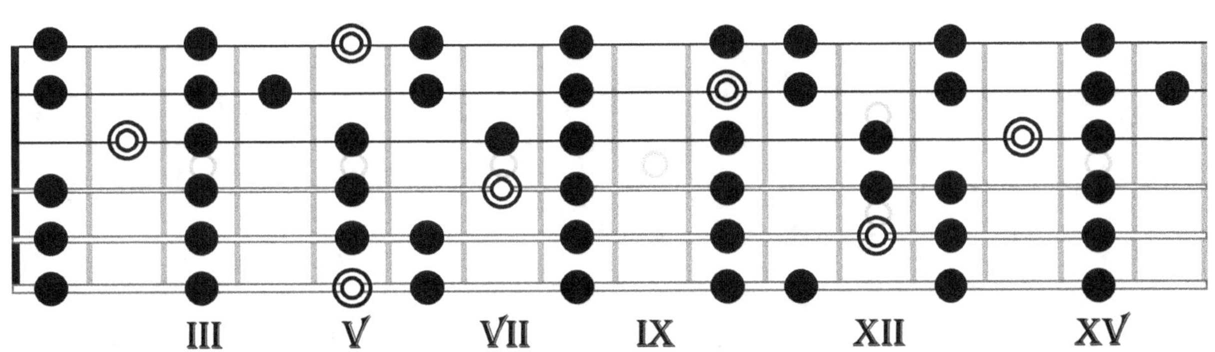

GUITAR SCALES: THE LOCRIAN MODE
BY LUCA MANCINO

A# LOCRIAN MODE

1 b2 b3 4 b5 b6 b7
A# B C# D# E F# G#

BOX 1

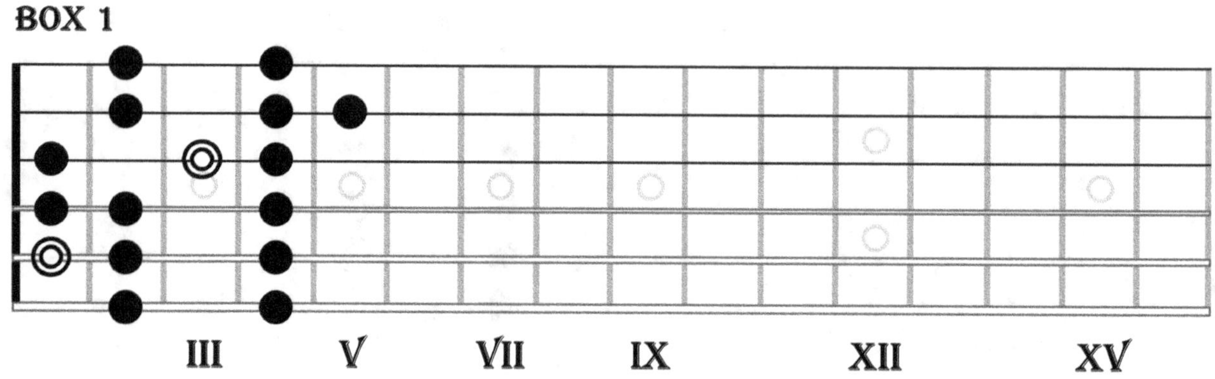

BOX 2

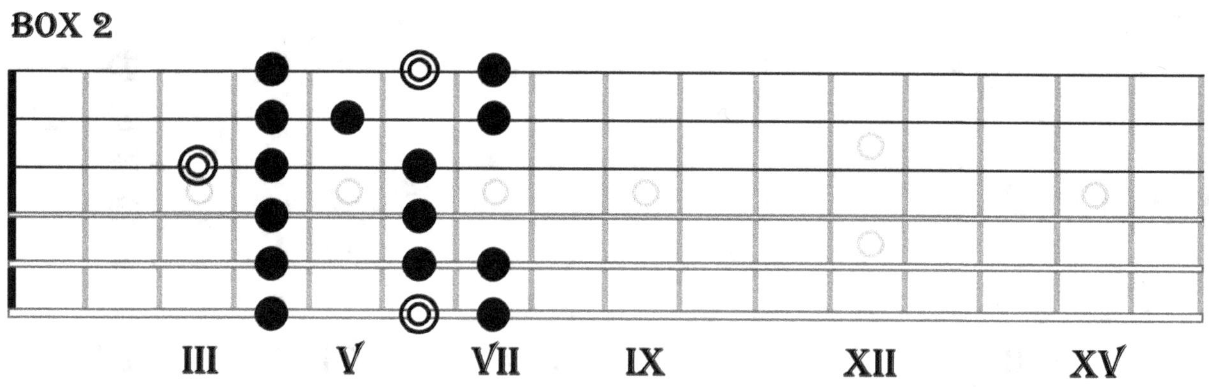

BOX 3

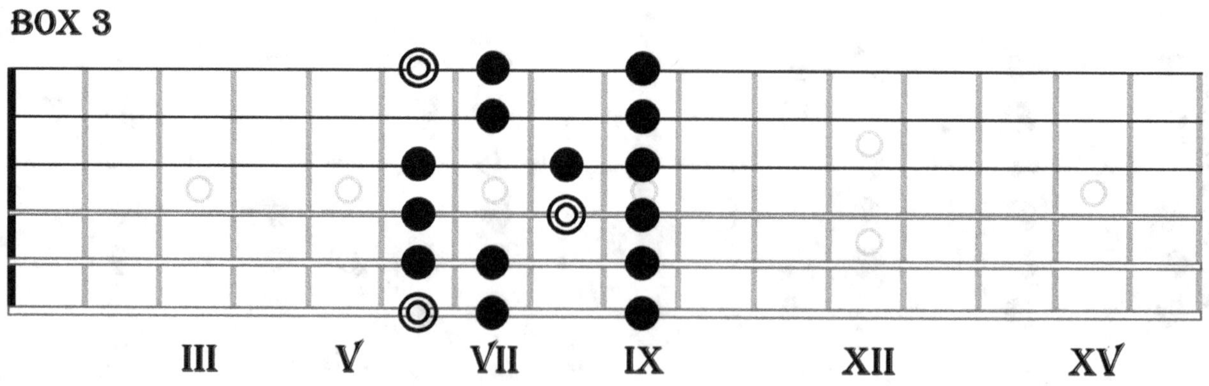

GUITAR SCALES: THE LOCRIAN MODE
BY LUCA MANCINO

BOX 4

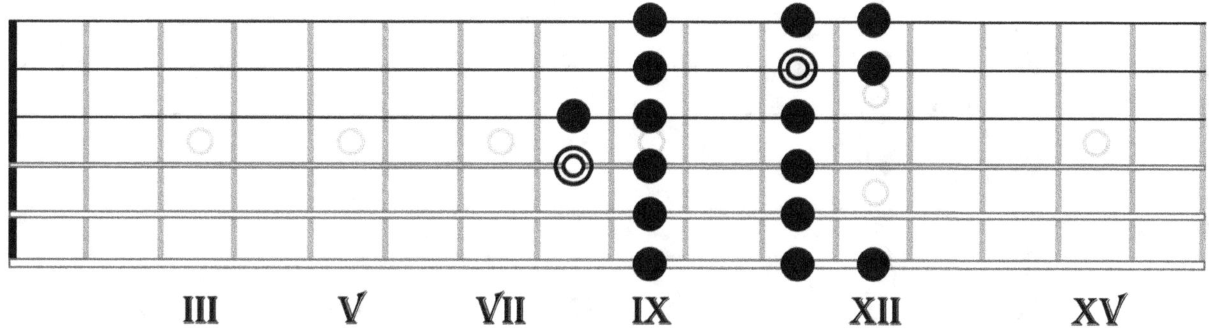

BOX 5

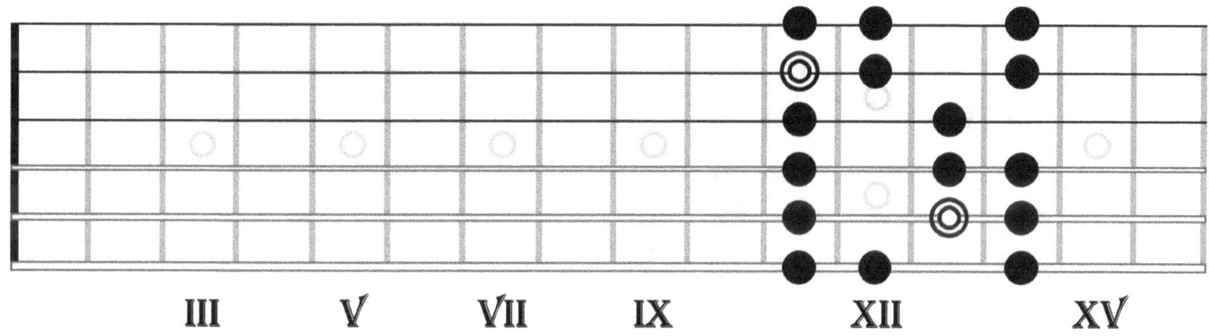

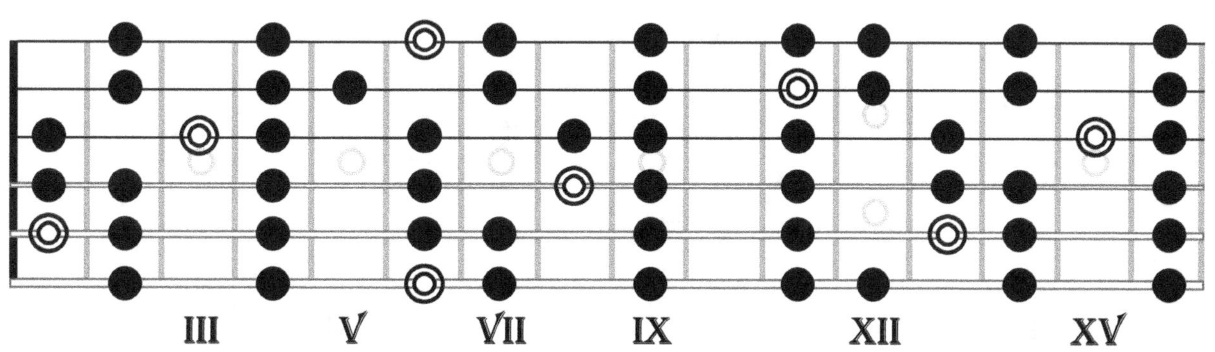

GUITAR SCALES: THE LOCRIAN MODE
BY LUCA MANCINO

B LOCRIAN MODE

1 b2 b3 4 b5 b6 b7
B C D E F G A

BOX 1

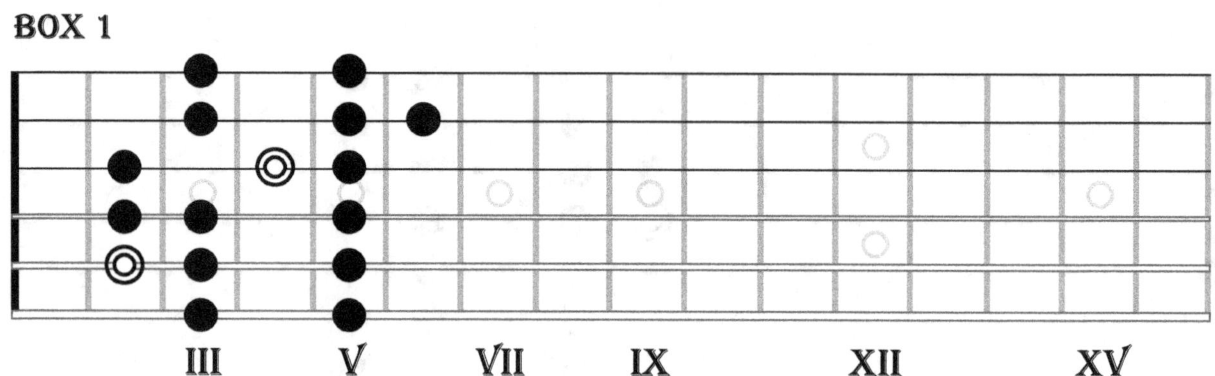

BOX 2

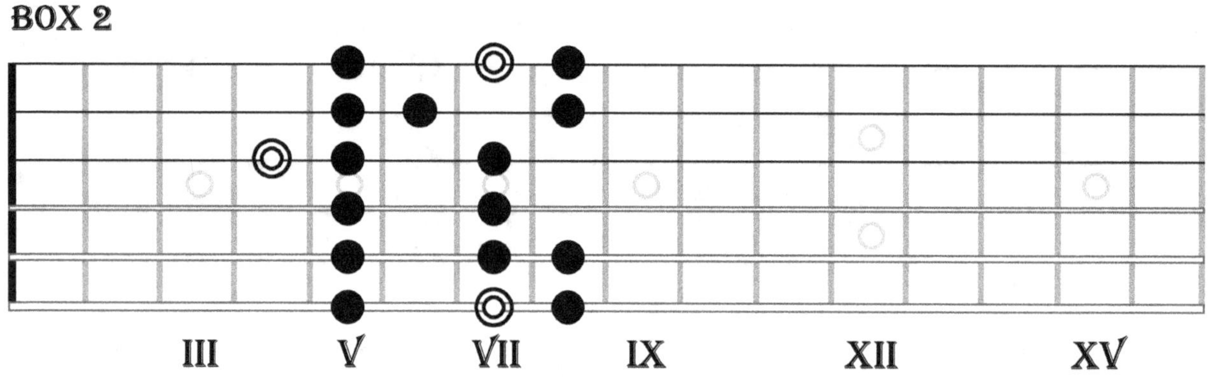

BOX 3

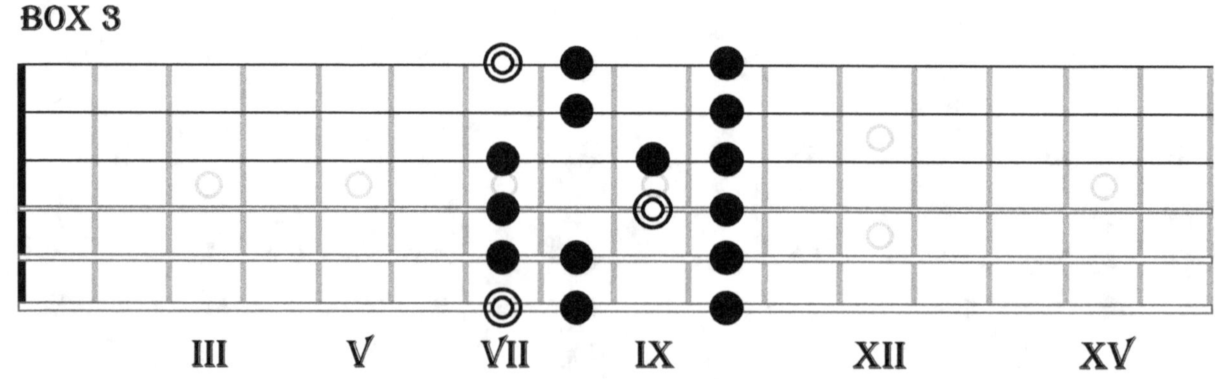

GUITAR SCALES: THE LOCRIAN MODE
BY LUCA MANCINO

BOX 4

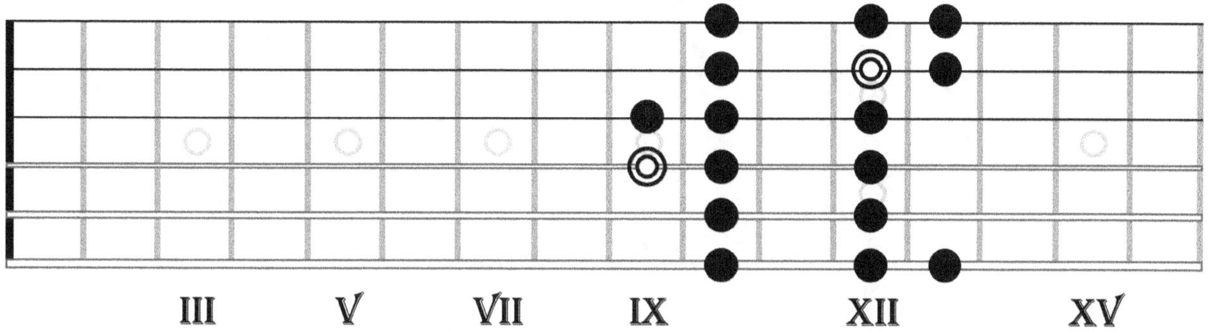

BOX 5

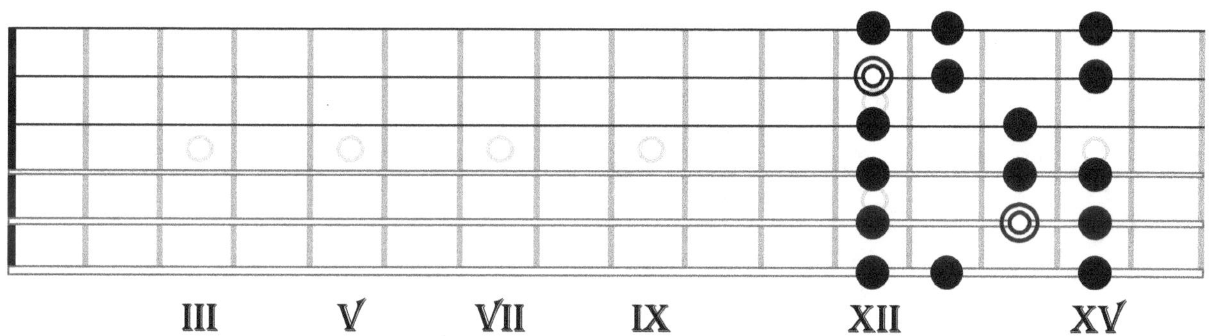

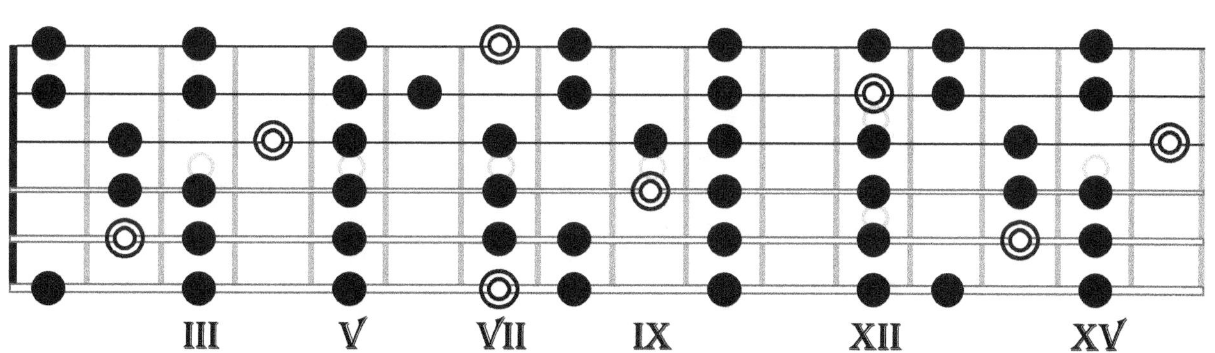

GUITAR SCALES: THE LOCRIAN MODE
BY LUCA MANCINO

GUITAR SCALES:

THE IONIAN MODE
THE DORIAN MODE
THE PHRYGIAN MODE
THE LYDIAN MODE
THE MIXOLYDIAN MODE
THE AEOLIAN MODE
THE LOCRIAN MODE
THE MAJOR PENTATONIC
THE MINOR PENTATONIC
THE MINOR BLUES
THE HARMONIC MINOR
THE MELODIC MINOR
THE PHRYGIAN DOMINANT
and many others…

BY

Nocera Inferiore (SA) - Italy
For contacts:
tel. + 39 348 3471854
e-mail: abmanagement@libero.it